FORTS IN AMERICA

SENTRY TOWER AT
THE CASTILLO DE SAN MARCOS

FORTS

Illustrated by DANIEL D. FEASER

HAROLD L. PETERSON

IN AMERICA

CHARLES SCRIBNER'S SONS, NEW YORK

791113151719 **MD/C** 2018161412108

PRINTED IN THE UNITED STATES OF AMERICA

SBN 684-12890-X

Library of Congress Catalog Card Number 64-17210

PENTAGONAL BRICK AND STONE REDOUBT
AT FORT PITT, 1765

Introduction

For almost four hundred years forts played a key role in American history. They were the first structures in each new colony along the Atlantic coast. This was often a hostile shore, and forts were needed for protection against both Indians and European rivals. As the frontier spread inland, the forts moved westward too. The selection of a defensible site often decided the location of settlements which have continued to the present day. Fort Pitt is now called Pittsburgh, but a large number of other cities and towns across the United States still carry the word "fort" in their names to indicate their origin.

Many kinds of forts have contributed to the growth of America. There have been fortified houses and missions, converted barns, factories or other buildings, and temporary field fortifications erected for a single campaign or perhaps even a single battle. Above all there have been the permanent forts. Designed specifically for defense and built to last, these permanent forts mirrored the growing knowledge and skill of their builders.

Literally hundreds of historic American forts still survive. They can be found in every state, and in most areas a short trip can include several that are open to the public as historic shrines. Visiting them can be a thrilling experience in reliving history. It can also lead to an appreciation of craftsmanship and of building techniques and to an insight into military science. The following pages trace the major developments in the design and construction of permanent forts in the United States.

STONE REDOUBT
INSIDE FORT NIAGARA, 1771

Contents

The Transition Period

The 1500's were years of change. The world had just been proved to be round. New continents had been discovered and awaited exploration and settlement. New trade routes to Africa and the Orient were bringing forth exotic materials and products. The last traces of feudalism were disappearing. Cities were growing larger and more important, and ways of life were altering rapidly.

Forts were changing too. The old castles were no longer safe strongholds against attack. Cannon had made them obsolete. These new and powerful guns could strike from a safe distance beyond the range of the archers or handgunners on the battlements. Castle walls were much too

Fort Caroline

high and thin to withstand the shattering impact of the cannon's solid iron balls. And castles were not designed to mount cannon of their own to help hold the attackers at bay. In 1494 King Charles VIII of France invaded Italy with a fine train of artillery, capturing cities almost at will. Castles that previously had held out for months fell in a few hours to the superior weapons. So complete was the domination of cannon over castle that for a time many people believed fortifications were no longer of any use.

Cooler heads, however, argued that although castles were indeed useless, new kinds of forts might be built which would offer efficient protection. During the 1500's engineers began to design such forts with lower, thicker walls made of soft materials that would not shatter easily. They put obstructions in front of the walls to prevent the enemy from getting a clear shot at the fort, and they added projections to the walls called bastions, so designed that cannon could be mounted in them to hold off the enemy in all directions.

These changes took time. For more than a hundred years engineers experimented with different designs and materials. During this period, which has been called the age of transition in fortification, the first forts in what is now the United States were built. They reflect the spirit of the times, for the settlers used available materials and sought to adapt the new designs to local situations.

One of the first American forts was Fort Caroline, near present-day Jacksonville, Florida. There a small colony of French Huguenots decided to establish a new home in 1564. The neighboring Indians seemed friendly at first, but the colonists were not sure how long this would last. Also, Spain claimed the territory they had selected. The Spaniards would look upon the French as trespassers and regard the settlement as a possible base for attacks against the treasure fleets which sailed up along the

FORT
CAROLINE

Florida coast on their way back to Spain. Thus the French knew they would need a strong fort for protection against either Spaniard or Indian, and it had to be big enough for the whole colony to live in.

The leader of the French settlement was René de Laudonnière. He was noted primarily as a mariner and ship captain, rather than as an expert in fortification, but the fort his men built was a good one. The site selected was a meadow suitable for a landing place on the banks of the St. Johns River. The fort itself was shaped like a triangle with its base on the river bank and its apex pointed inland.

To start, the colonists dug a deep ditch along the two land sides of the triangle and let water from the river flow in to form a moat. Curious Indians helped in the labor. The dirt from the ditch was piled along its inside edge to make a wall or rampart 9 feet high along the land sides of the fort. Military engineers had learned that dirt was one of the most effective defenses against cannon. Balls that could shatter a stone wall simply buried themselves in the dirt.

Dirt, however, would erode and wash away in heavy rains, and so it had to be faced with something to hold it in place. For the inside facing the French tied bundles of sticks together to make fascines. These they fastened to the dirt walls by driving stakes through them. They also put a layer of fascines crosswise through the dirt wall every 2 or 3 feet to help hold it together. For the outside facing they used sod. Turf was cut into blocks and laid up along the outside wall in much the same manner as a mason would lay bricks, except that stakes were used to fasten the blocks in place instead of mortar. In laying sod, the grass side was always placed down. This kept the dirt from shaking out, and soon the grass would grow out and up the sides of the wall, holding the dirt firmly in place to make a strong defense.

The side of the fort towards the river was different. There the French built a stockade wall of sawn planks, heavily braced and probably pierced with loopholes so they could shoot through it. Apparently Laudonnière planned to rely on his ships to prevent an attack on the fort from this direction, for this was the weakest wall. The strong sides faced the land.

Along the inside of the dirt walls the French built a wide ledge to stand on. In the event of an attack they could fire over the thin upper part of

the wall or parapet. At each of the three angles of the walls they built a bastion. These were also roughly triangular in shape, with widened ledges to provide room for mounting cannon. Because of the way these ledges were designed, the cannon could only be placed to cover the land faces of the fort, another indication that this was the direction from which Laudonnière expected an attack. Later bastions would offer much wider and more versatile coverage, but Fort Caroline was an early experiment with such devices. Improvements came with time and experience.

On the land wall to the right the French built the only entrance to the fort. They made a dirt bridge or causeway across the moat, and over the heavy wooden doors they erected a tall archway with the arms of France carved proudly at the top. It was the only handsome decoration in the simple fort.

Inside the walls were the necessary structures for daily living. This was to be a permanent colony with men, women and children from all walks of life—nobles, artisans, scholars, and the artist Jacques Le Moyne who painted pictures of the colony. There were simple houses thatched with palm leaves for the citizens and the soldiers and a bigger house for

The Spanish attack

Laudonnière. Because they had never seen a Florida hurricane, the French built one of the houses too tall, and it was promptly blown down. Thereafter the houses were made lower and stronger. Fort Caroline also contained a guardhouse, a granary, an arms magazine and other storehouses. And there was a well for water. There were some buildings outside the fort too, including a bake oven which was placed away from the houses to avoid the danger of fire. In an emergency, however, all necessary cooking could be done inside the fort, and the outer buildings could be abandoned.

Except for the river front, Fort Caroline was strong; yet it did not survive. On a rainy night in September, 1565, the Spanish struck. Most of the French fighting men were away on an expedition against the Spanish settlement of St. Augustine. Because of the wet weather the sentries had foolishly been allowed to stay inside where it was warm and dry. In the confusion of the sudden attack, someone opened the gate, and the Spaniards poured in to overwhelm such resistance as Laudonnière could organize among the remaining French. A few men and women managed to escape, but most were either captured or killed. The Spanish conquerors strengthened the fort and renamed it Fort San Mateo, but in 1568 the French took revenge and destroyed it completely. Today even the site is gone, washed away by the St. Johns River. Fort Caroline National Memorial on the present river bank commemorates its dramatic history.

In 1607, within fifty years of the destruction of Fort Caroline, English colonists built a triangular fort at Jamestown, Virginia. Unlike the Indians near Fort Caroline, those in Virginia were definitely hostile. When the English first set foot ashore, the Indians attacked and wounded several of them. Thus the new colonists' immediate project, after they had selected the site for their settlement, was the building of a fort. They anchored their ships late on May 13, began work on the fort the next day and finished it by mid-June. It was quick work, but they knew they needed protection against both the Indians and the Spanish who also claimed Virginia as their own.

No one knows who designed the fort at Jamestown. Captain John Smith arrived as a prisoner in irons because of an argument on board

JAMESTOWN

15

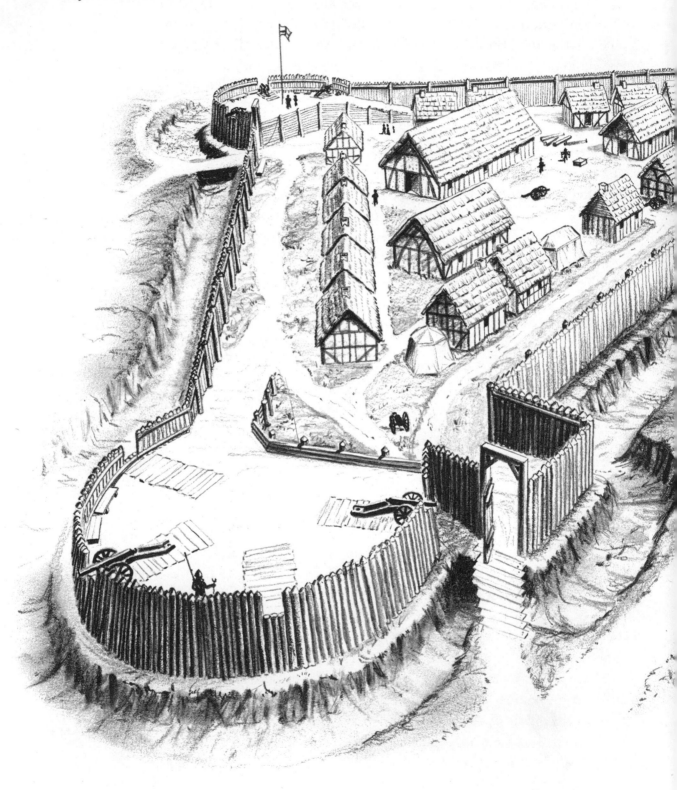

The fort at Jamestown, 1607

ship and he was not freed until the fort was almost finished. Thus in all probability he had little or nothing to do with it. The designer may have been Edward Maria Wingfield since he was the only other leader of wide military experience and since he also was president of the council that governed the colony. In any event, the new fort was similar to Fort Caroline in two ways. It was built on a river bank to protect the ship anchorage, and it was triangular in form with its base towards the river and its apex pointed inland.

There the similarities ceased. A ditch was dug all around the fort at Jamestown, even on the river front; but because the river bank was high, it was a dry ditch rather than a wet moat. In fact, a dry ditch was almost as good a protection as a wet one. It was made so wide that an attacking party could not reach the actual wall from the outer rim. If the enemy did manage to get down into the ditch, he found the top of the wall that much higher above his head, and the time it took him to climb in or out of this obstacle exposed him that much longer to the fire of the defenders.

The English built all of the walls at Jamestown of wood. A stockade of logs, planks and posts 14 or 15 feet high was erected. Not as strong as the dirt walls of Fort Caroline, but more resilient than stone, the wooden walls were probably heavy enough to withstand shots from small cannon.

At each corner of the triangle formed by the stockade was a bastion just as there was at Fort Caroline. At Jamestown, however, the bastions were circular, much as if their designer had been thinking of the round towers of castles. These bastions were the principal defensive positions in the fort. Dirt from the ditch was probably used to raise the floor level of the bastions to within 5 or 6 feet of the top of the stockade. Here most of the cannon were mounted, and a firing step would have been built between the openings for the big guns so that the soldiers could shoot over the top of the wall. From these

Cannon were hauled up dirt ramps to the bastions

positions the men could cover the long "curtains" as the walls between the bastions were called.

The English built several gates at Jamestown. The main gate was in the center of the wall towards the river, and there were smaller ones on the land sides right next to the bastions. Each entrance was defended by a cannon mounted inside directly facing the gate. There were probably loopholes for small arms too, although the records are not clear about this.

This was a big fort. The river front was 140 yards long, and each of the other sides was 100 yards. Like Fort Caroline, Jamestown contained all the buildings necessary for survival in case of attack: a storehouse, guardhouse and market place and, perhaps most important, the well for water. Even the bake oven was inside, and this may have been a mistake for there were a number of fires. Along each land wall was a row of small thatched houses, and in the center of the fort was a big church which John Smith described as "a homely thing like a barne."

Within the walls of Jamestown the first permanent English settlement in America eked out its early years. Life in the fort was harsh, and survival was a matter of luck. Most of the settlers were men. There were very few women in the beginning and almost no comforts. Disease, crop failures and hostile Indians plagued the little band. The winter of 1609–1610 brought the "Starving Time" when all of these ills reached their peak. In a few short months death reduced the population from about 500 to 60, and the few survivors were so weak they could hardly care for themselves.

Spring brought some relief. More settlers arrived under the leadership of Sir Thomas Gates. He was shocked at the appearance of the fort. It looked, he wrote, "rather as the ruins of some ancient fortification, then that any people living might now inhabit it." The stockade posts and some of the houses had been used for firewood by colonists too weak to gather fuel in the forest or too fearful of the Indians who lurked nearby. Indeed the Indians could have captured the village at almost any time, so poorly was it protected. For some reason they never tried, perhaps believing that it was to their advantage to wait until starvation and disease had claimed even more defenders. Within a month of Gates's arrival another group of colonists came with the new governor, Lord Delaware. The crisis was past, and the settlement was firmly established.

The fort at Jamestown was never attacked although Spanish spies quickly provided their king with a map and a description. Still, its life was almost the same length as Fort Caroline's. From 1607 until 1610 it was the heart of the colony. Then with the increase of population the settlement began to spread out. Newer defenses were built further away, and the first fort disappeared. Its timbers rotted, and the colonists undoubtedly leveled the bastions and filled the ditches. Today the original site has been washed away by the James River, but there is an excellent model of it in the visitor center of Colonial National Historical Park at Jamestown. Nearby, the State of Virginia has erected a full-scale reconstruction which gives a very accurate impression of this early fort if one remembers that the ditch should be larger and the stockade higher.

PLYMOUTH   More relaxed militarily than either of their southern neighbors were the Pilgrims who landed at Plymouth, Massachusetts, in December, 1620. They were primarily tradespeople, farmers and artisans with little military experience or inclination. The Indians were few, and the Spanish were far away. It was up to doughty little Miles Standish, their military adviser, to take charge of such matters. Under his direction, the Pilgrims' first effort for defense was a simple but stout stockade enclosing the houses and gardens which were given primary attention. The palisade with three gates was completed in March, 1621. It had no bastions but would have afforded some protection against a surprise Indian attack. Standish was careful to see that a watch was kept at all times and that the gates were locked at night.

This first stockade was a simple wall of logs about 8 feet tall. A few years later a more complicated wall was built. It was made of planks 9 feet long, sharpened at the top and fastened to a framework of stout posts, 10 inches in diameter, set 19 feet apart and connected with three cross rails.

Plymouth with its fortifications complete

20

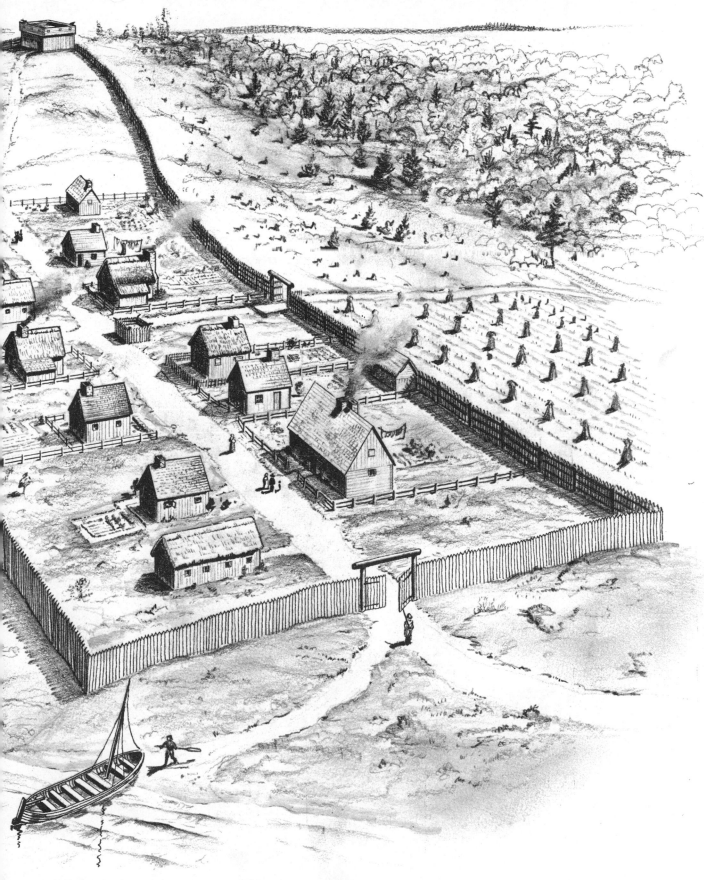

Both walls were well built. They might be climbed, but it would take a heavy blow to knock them down. John Pory of Jamestown, who visited Plymouth in 1622, described the first one as "stronger than I have seene anie in Virginia."

At the time of Pory's visit, the Pilgrims were also at work on their first true fort. This was a square blockhouse of heavy oak timbers with a flat roof and battlements for mounting four heavy cannon. The ground floor of the building, which was pierced with loopholes for small arms, was used as a church and meeting house and also provided sleeping quarters for the guard. The site selected for the fort was the top of a hill, the highest ground in the vicinity. From it the cannon could cover the entire harbor and keep enemy ships away. Since the village itself was further down the slope of the hill, the stockade was extended to the fort and then back, making a wall 2,700 feet long. The building thus became a form of bastion or redoubt at the angle of two curtain walls. In a sense it was the ancestor of a whole host of later frontier forts composed of blockhouses and a stockade.

Defensive arrangements were completed with the erection of a small square stockade in the center of the village where the two streets crossed. Four little swivel guns mounted there could cover the streets and gates in every direction.

Planks for the fort were cut in a saw pit

The fort at Plymouth

The Plymouth fortifications were not particularly strong even when complete. They would have withstood a short attack, but a siege would quickly have captured them. There was only one blockhouse. Two or more would have offered protection to each other. The stockade, though stout, was too long and too low to be defended adequately, and as far as surviving records show, there were no loopholes or other provisions for shooting through or over it. All it offered was an obstacle that would slow an attacking force and perhaps allow the colonists time to run to the fort where they might huddle together with some safety until their food and water ran out.

Fortunately for the Pilgrims, the defenses were never tested. With periodic repairs the fortifications stood until they were no longer needed and the timber was used to build houses. The site of the original Pilgrim fort remains in the center of the burial ground at Plymouth while the modern city covers the area within the stockade. On a similar site just outside the city, however, Plimoth Plantation, Inc. has reconstructed the original village and its fortifications so that it is still possible to see and test the strengths and weaknesses of a pioneer blockhouse and stockade system.

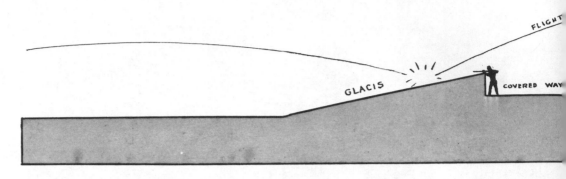

The Bastioned System

While colonists from England, France and Spain built simple forts in the wilds of North America, military engineers of Europe worked at perfecting a whole system of fortification. Each nation developed slightly different versions of its own, but two men are generally recognized as having brought the new system to its highest development. One was a Frenchman, Marshal Sebastien le Prestre de Vauban (1633–1707); the other a Hollander, Baron Menno van Coehoorn (1641–1704). Each of them published a set of general principles for fortification, and each supervised the construction of great defensive systems within his own country. For over a hundred years almost every other military engineer in Europe described his own ideas about fortification by comparing them with the work of these two men.

The key features of the new system were the perfection of the bastions of the main fort and the development of a series of outerworks designed to keep the enemy and his cannon balls away from the fort itself. It was the bastion which gave the system its name, but the outer defenses were just as important.

There had been bastions at Fort Caroline, at Jamestown and at other forts in America during the 1500's and early 1600's, but they were largely experimental and inefficient. In the new system the fort was usually a four- or five-sided structure with a pointed bastion at each corner designed so that every foot of ground immediately surrounding the fort could be covered by the fire of the defenders. There was no "dead space" where an attacker would be safe from harm because the guns of the fort could not be pointed at him.

The outerworks began at the ditch. Instead of throwing all of the dirt along the inside edge of the ditch to form the fort walls, the builders put some on the outside as well. Thus they created a bank with a steep inner

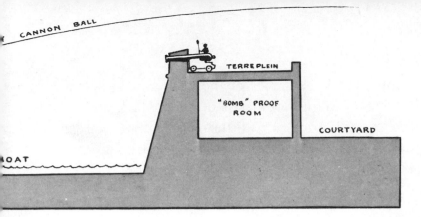

Cross section of the wall and outworks of a typical bastioned fort

face and an outer surface that sloped gradually away. This slope was called the glacis, and it had several purposes. First of all, it was high enough to protect the lower part of the fort's rampart from enemy fire. Cannon balls striking the sloping surface might even bounce right over the fort, missing it entirely. Second, it created a smooth field all around with no bumps or gullies in which an attacker might hide. Finally, it afforded protection for an advanced line of defenders. This was done by leaving a ledge between the ditch and the steep inner bank of the glacis. Soldiers could stand on this ledge, or covered way as it was called, and use the bank as a breastwork. An attacking force would have to drive them out of this advanced position before it could even think of assaulting the main fort.

There were more formal outworks also. The most important was a triangular defense called a ravelin or demilune. These ravelins were built at the outer edge of the ditch and were designed to protect a gateway by cutting off enemy fire. They might also be used to cover the curtain wall between the bastions on those sides of a fort from which an attack was most likely.

Other outworks included separate small forts called redoubts. Sometimes these were actually blockhouses, sometimes just dirt embankments erected outside the glacis, perhaps as much as a musket shot away. Redoubts were designed to slow up the advance of an enemy and give the defenders of the main fort as much time as possible to get ready. There were defenses with jagged outlines called horn works and crown works and many more besides. In Europe whole cities and harbors were ringed with miles of such fortifications, but in America there was seldom more than the principal fort with its bastions, ditch, glacis, one or two ravelins and perhaps a redoubt. For the wild new country this was usually enough.

THE CASTILLO
DE
SAN MARCOS

One of the most beautiful early examples of the bastioned system in America is the Castillo de San Marcos or Castle of Saint Mark built by the Spanish at St. Augustine, Florida. The little outpost that guarded the route of the treasure ships needed a stout defense. France and England both envied the wealth Spain received from her colonies. Free-

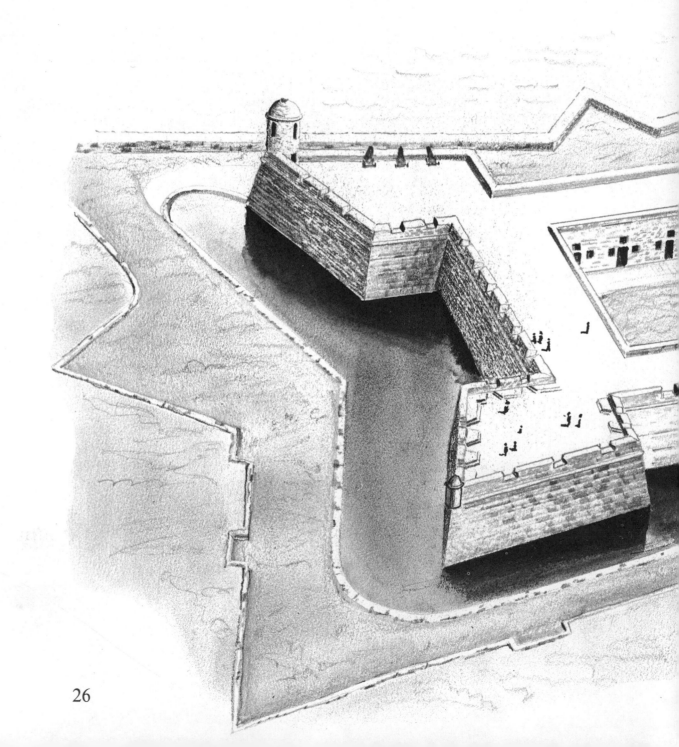

booters, pirates and privateers delighted in capturing the gold, silver and gems carried by Spanish ships or stored in Spanish warehouses. St. Augustine itself was a poor town with no wealth to tempt the pirates, but it offered a haven for the ships, and so it was raided time and time again, once by Sir Francis Drake. Nine wood and dirt forts were built one after

The Castillo de San Marcos as it appears today

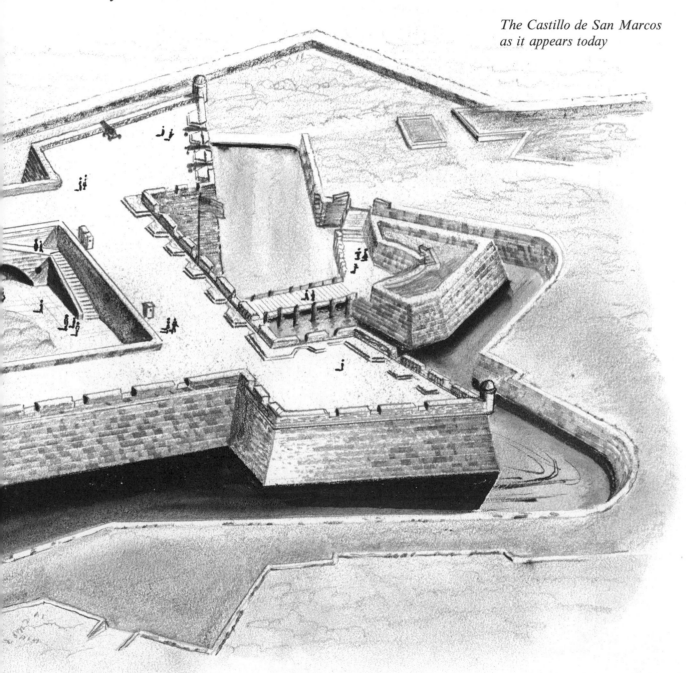

another to protect the town, but the soil was sandy and eroded easily and wood rotted quickly in the damp climate. Indians burned one fort, the English destroyed another, and the rest fell apart by themselves. Something more permanent was needed.

On October 2, 1672, Don Manuel de Sendoya, governor and captain general of the province, turned the first shovelful of earth to mark the beginning of a new stone fort. Ignacio Daza, a military engineer, had designed it in the latest fashion. It was to be a stout defense with four bastions, a moat, covered way and glacis. There would be a ravelin too,

The soft coquina was quarried with pick and crowbar

Sentry tower at the Castillo de San Marcos

directly in front of the gate, and anyone who wanted to enter would have to cross the moat twice. One drawbridge would lead him to the ravelin; a longer one would take him to the fort itself. Even then he would be faced by heavy doors and a portcullis—a grating of stout timbers shod with iron that could be raised and lowered to form a second door. A surprise assault would be all but impossible if the garrison was alert, and to provide shelter for the sentries, little watchtowers were built on the point of each bastion. Inside the fort there were quarters for the soldiers, storerooms for provisions and ammunition, a well, a prison and a chapel.

Daza and the Governor selected the site for the fort carefully. Built on the shore of Matanzas Bay, it could defend the harbor; and a shallow sand bar kept big ships far enough away so that their heavy guns could not reach the fort. Swamps, arms of the bay and a creek protected the other sides of the Castillo, making it difficult for an enemy to bring siege guns against it.

The Castillo de San Marcos took many years to build. Spanish workmen, Indians and prisoners quarried the soft native shell rock called coquina and built the walls 30 feet high and up to 12 feet thick for wages that ranged from 12½¢ a day for a laborer to $3 a day for the engineer. Daza died, and new governors replaced Sendoya, but the work continued for almost twenty-five years before the fort was completed. Even then there were improvements to follow as new engineers added bombproof rooms and strengthened some of the outworks. Finally the fort was finished, a massive structure, impregnable in its day—and handsome. The white plaster which covered all its walls reflected the strong Florida sun and contrasted with the red watchtowers and the painted decorations inside, while the waters of the moat mirrored the sculptured arms of Spain above the entrance.

The Castillo needed all its strength. Pirates, Indians, English soldiers and American colonists all attacked it. There were raids in 1683, 1704, 1728 and 1743 and actual sieges in 1702 and 1740.

General James Oglethorpe, governor of the new English colony of Georgia, conducted the second siege and gave the Castillo its severest test. Because the fort was so well-placed, the English could get their artillery no closer than the far side of the bay. From that distance their big guns thundered at the fort for twenty-seven straight days. But the soft shell rock did not splinter under the impact of the heavy iron balls. Instead, it absorbed them as one Englishman remarked, "as though you would stick a knife into cheese." Only two Spaniards in the fort were killed. Discouraged, Oglethorpe quit the bombardment. He thought about a direct assault but abandoned that idea and decided to starve out the garrison. Finally he gave that up too, and on the thirty-eighth day of the siege he sailed back to Georgia.

After the raid of 1743, the rest of the Castillo's days were relatively peaceful. England gained control of the fort by treaty in 1763, kept American prisoners there during the Revolution, and by the treaty ending that war returned it to Spain in 1783.

In 1821 the United States acquired Florida from Spain, and the Castillo was renamed Fort Marion after General Francis Marion. In 1924 it became a National Monument, and it still stands today for all who wish to see this fine original example of the early bastioned system of fortification.

One of the principal teachings of Marshal Vauban was that a fort should not be built according to rigid rules. He believed that the theories of fortification should be modified and adapted to the nature of the ground and the place to be defended. Canadian-born Lt. Michel Chartier, Sieur de Lotbinière, studied military engineering in France and had Vauban's instruction clearly in mind when he set out, in 1755, to build one of America's great bastioned forts in the wilderness along the shores of Lake Champlain. He named his project Fort Vaudreuil at first, then Fort Carillon. Later the English called it Fort Ticonderoga. De Lotbinière selected the crest of a rocky ridge at the base of a peninsula that jutted out into the lake. From this position he could command a key point—the main route to Lake George. The steep slopes to the lake protected the

*Plan of Fort Ticonderoga
and its outworks*

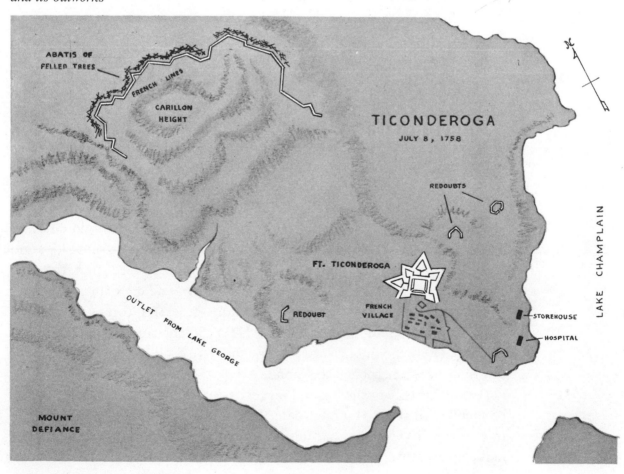

fort from attack on two sides, but made ditching in the usual manner impossible. The solid rock just beneath the earth's surface hampered ditching on the other sides. De Lotbinière had to do something different.

The first year he could do little more than clear the land and make a modest start. He outlined a typical four-bastioned fort with ravelins or demilunes protecting the curtain walls on the two sides from which an enemy might attack. His men raised the walls to a height of 7 feet before most of them had to leave for winter quarters.

This was not a stone-faced fort in the beginning. De Lotbinière had no stonemasons and few tools. Thus he built the walls of horizontal logs and dirt. To do this he constructed two log walls about 10 feet apart, fastened together by crosspieces. The space between was filled with rubble and dirt. It was an ancient technique and many American forts were built in this manner, including Fort William Henry at the southern end of Lake George. There the English and Americans were establishing a base hoping to drive the French back to Canada.

One advantage of the log and dirt construction was that it could always be faced with stone at a later date. This was exactly what the French did in 1756 and 1757 as they continued work on the fort. Stone facings helped make a fort stronger and more durable. Even if the stone shattered even-

*Fort Ticonderoga as it
appears today*

tually under cannon fire, the dirt behind remained as a solid protection.
And the stone held the dirt in place, preventing erosion and simplifying
maintenance. At this time the French also raised the height of the walls,
and then started on the outworks.

A wall was built along one steep slope a little way from the fort to
provide a breastwork and a place to mount cannon. A covered way was
planned for the other steep side, but it was never completed. Instead, the
French concentrated on the two exposed sides. They completed two
large demilunes and dug a ditch around them. It was a most unusual
ditch. The workmen just cut away part of the low hillside in front of the
fort, blasting out rock to clear the way. Thus the bottom of the ditch was
on the same level as the parade ground inside, and the main entrance
opened right into it. The natural hill made a perfect glacis. De Lotbinière
had obeyed the master Vauban well in changing his plans to fit the ground.
Out towards the end of the point the young French engineer built a redoubt. Other small works to protect approaches to the fort and to guard
important places were added later.

33

Inside the fort were the usual necessary storerooms and living quarters. Interestingly, the barracks towered over the walls, and other engineers were critical of this for the buildings thus became targets for enemy cannon. The well was outside the fort too. Set on one of the protected sides, it probably would have been accessible even during an attack. Just to be sure, however, the French built a big cistern to collect and store rainwater so that they would have a supply even if the well were cut off.

Ticonderoga was an excellent fortification, well designed and well built. But it took more than that for a fort to be impregnable. Much depended upon the skill and determination of the attackers and defenders—and upon the number of men available. The history of Fort Ticonderoga—one successful defense and three captures—points this out very clearly. In none of the encounters was the strength of the fort itself questioned.

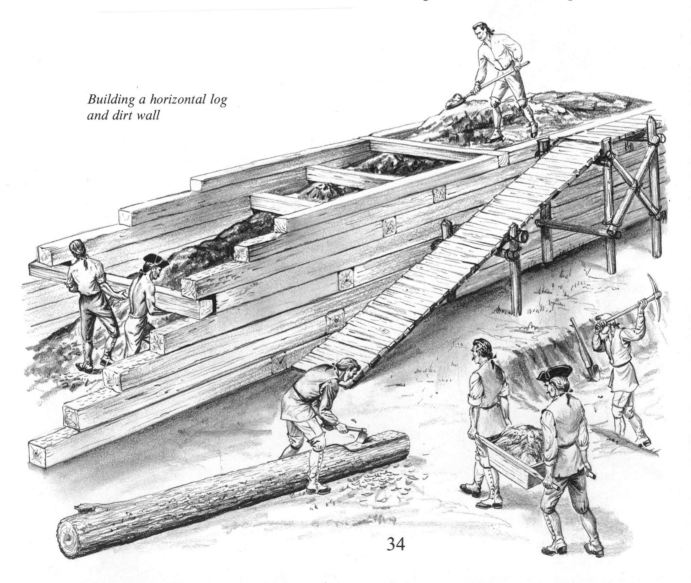

Building a horizontal log and dirt wall

34

Redoubt No. 10 at Yorktown,
a dirt fortification
with horizontal log fraises

The first attack against Ticonderoga was launched by a British and American army in 1758. The French, commanded by the renowned Marquis de Montcalm, met them at an entrenched line well in front of the fort and defeated them decisively. Then the fortunes of war changed. When a new British-American army returned the next year, Montcalm and most of the French army were away. The remaining garrison resisted the attackers for a few days, then blew up the powder magazine, set fire to the fort and retreated without really trying to defend it.

The British rebuilt the fort, officially named it Fort Ticonderoga, and then proceeded to lose it just as quickly and ignominiously as the French had. The American Revolution broke out in April, 1775, but news traveled slowly in such remote areas. Ethan Allen and Benedict Arnold with only eighty-three Green Mountain Boys were able to surprise and capture the great fort because its commander did not even know there was a war.

This victory gave the Americans their chance to make a mistake. They failed to fortify a steep hill overlooking the fort because they did not believe an enemy could possibly haul cannon up its slopes. In 1777, however, a British Army under General John Burgoyne mounted guns on the hill and 3,000 American troops had to flee for their lives, leaving the fort to the British. Later that year a surprise raid by the Americans under Colonel John Brown captured most of the outworks but failed to retake the fort.

At the end of the American Revolution the British abandoned Fort Ticonderoga, and it was never again occupied by a military garrison. Today the great fort has been restored through the efforts of the late Stephen H. P. Pell and the Fort Ticonderoga Association, and it is possible once more to see just how the young de Lotbinière adapted a bastioned fort to fit a special situation.

There were many bastioned forts built in America. Some were stone like the Castillo de San Marcos or dirt faced with stone like Fort Ticonderoga. Some had only dirt walls. Others like Fort William Henry used the horizontal log and dirt wall construction, and some combined that with the vertical palisade. Many used the palisade alone. The design of a fort was determined by its strategic importance, the speed with which it had to be built, the materials and skilled labor available to the engineer.

Most forts were four-sided, but there were also some with five sides and five bastions. Fort Pitt was one, Fort Ontario at Oswego, New York,

Fort McHenry, 1814

was another, and Fort McHenry in Maryland was a third. All had similar outlines, but there the likeness ceased. Fort Ontario was of log and dirt construction. Fort Pitt, with one of the finest systems of outworks ever built in America, was primarily a dirt fort except that the two most exposed sides were faced with masonry.

Fort McHenry, much the latest of the three, had all of its dirt walls faced with brick both inside and out. This famous fort guarding Baltimore harbor was built between 1794 and 1805 and named for James McHenry, Secretary of War. Later years brought modifications designed to increase its strength. It had one ravelin opposite its entrance and a ditch all the way around. Since its main purpose was to protect the harbor, additional batteries of cannon with dirt embankments for protection were erected close to the shore. These could be abandoned if necessary, and the artillerists could flee into the main fort.

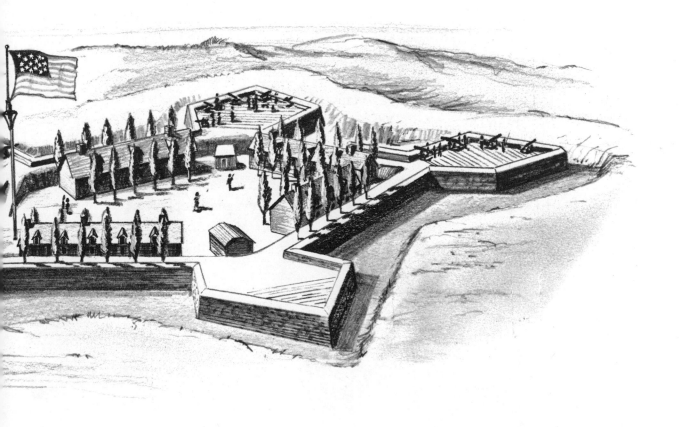

Fortunately Fort McHenry was solidly built. When the British attacked Baltimore in September, 1814, their ships had guns with a longer range than those in the fort. They stopped out of range of the Americans and bombarded them with rockets and huge mortar shells. Major George Armistead and his garrison in the fort were helpless to reply. All day long the British kept up their fire. Then, at night, they tried to send a party upriver past the fort to land behind it. At last the Americans could shoot back, and they did so with vigor, aiming at the flashes of the British guns. They shot well and the British fell back.

On the deck of a British ship in the harbor Francis Scott Key watched the shelling. He had come aboard to seek the release of a prominent Baltimore physician and was detained by the British for the duration of the battle. Keeping an anxious vigil through the night, Key wondered if his countrymen could possibly stand the pounding. When dawn broke and he saw the huge flag still flying over the fort, he took a letter from his pocket and wrote a few lines of a poem to express his joy and gratitude. Later that day the British gave up their attack, and Key went ashore. He completed his poem, and it was printed as a handbill in Baltimore on September 15, 1814. He called it "Defence of Fort McHenry," but it soon became known as "The Star-Spangled Banner."

Fort McHenry weathered the bombardment well. Major Armistead estimated that perhaps as many as 1,800 shells had been fired by the British and that about 400 had actually landed within his defenses. One gun had been disabled; two buildings had been damaged; four Americans had been killed and twenty-four wounded. But the strong fort walls had survived, and so had the nerves of the defenders. Today the ditch and the water batteries are gone and some heavy gun emplacements of the Civil War era are scattered about, but Fort McHenry itself, now a unit in the National Park System, still stands solidly at the edge of Baltimore harbor.

Erecting a log stockade

The Forts Move West

Big bastioned forts like Ticonderoga, McHenry and the Castillo de San Marcos were designed to withstand attacks by European enemies with heavy artillery. They guarded important cities and transportation routes such well-equipped foes might attack. In the back country where big bodies of troops and heavy guns could not move so readily, forts could be simpler. Here the principal enemies were Indians and perhaps a few hostile white men. There would probably be no artillery to worry about, and the chances of a long siege would be slight. Indians did not normally fight that way.

Blockhouse with octagonal top,
Fort Vancouver, Washington, c. 1846

For the remote hamlet, the trading post or the frontier Army garrison, blockhouses and stockades were the standard defenses. Occasionally such fortifications were made of stone. Sir William Johnson had two stone blockhouses to protect his estate at Johnstown, New York, and Fort Snelling, Minnesota, boasted stone walls as well as a blockhouse and tower. But these were exceptions. Wood was the usual material. In most places there was plenty of timber waiting to be cut. It was easier to use than stone, and it was strong enough to withstand the type of attack that could be expected.

The Pilgrims had made their second stockade of sawn plank, but most American frontier forts were built of whole logs. If there was time, the pioneers would square the logs with axes so that they would fit together more tightly, and the War Department recommended in 1803 that logs used in Army forts be peeled and burned slightly so that they would last longer.

Some of the frontier forts were extremely simple. For the smallest a single blockhouse was sometimes thought to be enough. Many others were only a little more elaborate. When the men of the famous Lewis and Clark expedition reached the Pacific coast in 1805 and realized that they would have to spend the winter in what is now Oregon, they built a little fort for protection against both Indians and the weather. On December 8 they began construction of two long low buildings facing each other and about 20 feet apart. By Christmas day the roofs were on, and the men celebrated by firing a volley from their guns, singing, exchanging simple gifts and feasting on lean elk meat, spoiled dried fish and roots. Then they went back to work and built stockade walls connecting the ends of the buildings. It was not much of a fort, but it was all they needed in that far-off place. They named it Fort Clatsop after a friendly Indian tribe.

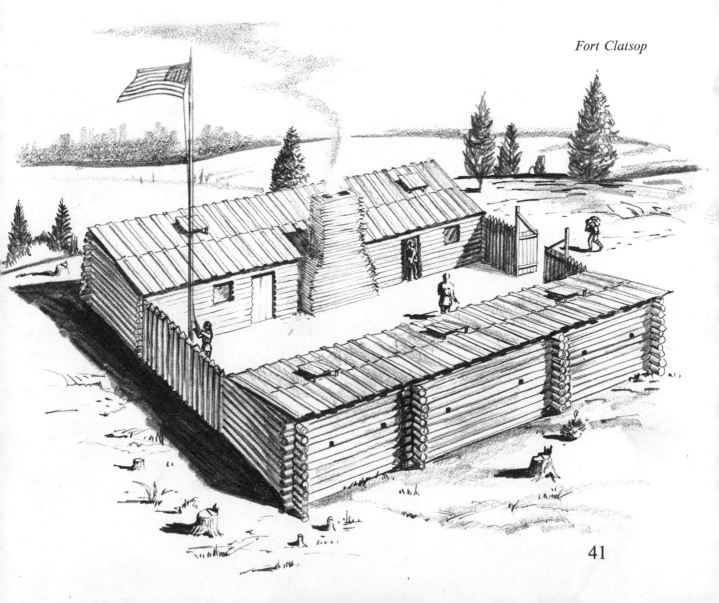

Fort Clatsop

The bigger and better forts usually had two blockhouses, tall stockades and several buildings inside. When these blockhouses were placed on diagonal corners of the walls and projected out beyond them, they served much the same functions as bastions in permitting the defenders to shoot along the outside of the stockade. Each blockhouse would cover two of the walls.

FORT
DEARBORN

Fort Dearborn was an excellent example of a fully developed frontier Army fort of the type preferred by the War Department about 1800. It was built by Captain John Whistler in 1803 at the foot of Lake Michigan. The site is now the city of Chicago, but at the time was occupied by only four huts.

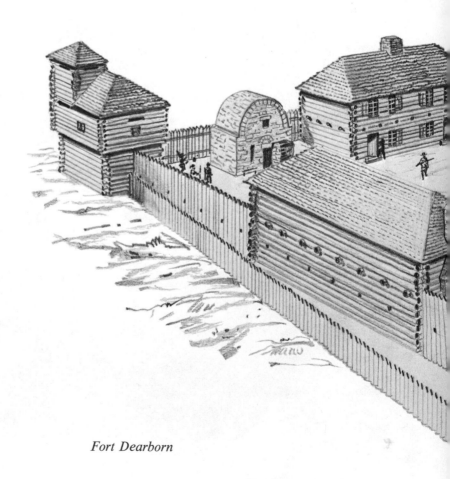

Fort Dearborn

The gallant captain had come to America with the British Army in 1777 to help subdue the rebellious colonies, but he had been captured at Saratoga and had grown to like the new land. When the war was over, he joined the American Army and proved a loyal and dependable soldier. Whistler built his fort in the wilderness precisely according to instructions from the War Department and even named it after Secretary of War Henry Dearborn. It had two blockhouses on diagonal corners and four large two-story buildings that formed a square. The space between these buildings was filled in with a stockade, and there were loopholes in both the back walls of the buildings and the stockade for the soldiers to shoot through. There were even two low stockade walls somewhat like bastions outside the main fort on the corners opposite the blockhouses to give the defenders more of a chance for a flanking fire along the walls. A special feature was a brick powder magazine, which Whistler's instructions had suggested he erect.

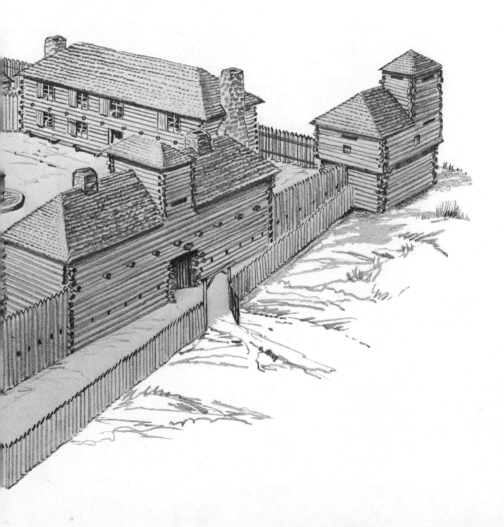

Fort Dearborn was everything that a frontier fort should be. Army specifications had been followed to the letter. But when the War of 1812 broke out, there were not enough supplies to maintain the fort and the commandant was ordered to abandon it and move the garrison and their families to Detroit. It was a sad mistake. Hostile Indians fell upon the departing residents, killed or captured almost all of them, and destroyed the fortification.

Fort William

FORT LARAMIE

One of the most famous of all Western frontier outposts was Fort Laramie. Located on the great Oregon Trail in what is now Wyoming, it was a depot for fur traders and trappers, a haven for emigrants and forty-niners, a station for the Pony Express and the Overland Stage, and an Army post. Jim Bridger, the famous mountain man, was a part-owner for a time. Kit Carson visited it. So did Calamity Jane and a host of other famous Westerners. Its history is a fine illustration of the evolution of America's Western forts.

Two fur traders, William Sublette and Robert Campbell, built the first Fort Laramie in 1834. They named it Fort William in honor of Sublette, but because of its position on the banks of the Laramie River, almost everyone called it Fort Laramie. Sublette and Campbell were experienced mountain men, and they built a good fort. They squared the timbers for the stockade and put blockhouses on diagonal corners. Over the gate they put another large blockhouse and mounted a cannon in it. In-

side they built rows of small cabins right up against the stockade so that their roofs formed a platform that defenders could stand on to shoot over the walls. Indians camped outside the walls in large numbers when they came to trade their furs for white men's goods. At such times the traders demonstrated their cannon with good effect. The artist Alfred Miller, who visited the fort in 1837, reported: "The Indians have a mortal horror of the 'big gun' which rests in the blockhouse, as they have had experience of its prowess and witnessed the havoc produced by its loud 'talk.'

Inside Fort William
(from a painting by Alfred Miller)

They conceive it to be only asleep and have a wholesome dread of its being waked up."

By 1841 the wooden walls of Fort William had decayed. A new fort was needed, and the Pierre Chouteau, Jr. and Company, which had bought the old fort, built a new one. Instead of logs they used adobe, a kind of sun-dried brick. Fort John, as they called it, also had two blockhouses, and its walls were 15 feet high with a little wooden palisade set on top for additional protection. Inside, the tops of the cabins still formed a firing platform. Trade with the Indians was good, and the Company also made a handsome profit selling supplies to westward-moving emigrants at exorbitant prices. The price for a cup of sugar, for instance, was $2, and bullets brought 75¢ a pound.

Fort John

Fort Laramie, 1876

As the emigrants moved West in greater numbers, the Army began to build forts to protect their routes of travel. In 1849 the War Department bought Fort John, and it became officially Fort Laramie. The old adobe fort was used for shelter at first, but almost immediately the soldiers began to erect buildings outside it in a square around an open parade ground. This became the Army post proper and the real Fort Laramie. By 1863 the old fort had vanished completely, and eventually even the minor defenses and outworks disappeared. Fort Laramie was a fort in name only. There were no walls or defenses of any kind.

These were active years for Fort Laramie. The Indians had become increasingly hostile. Councils were held in efforts to obtain peace, and when these failed and open warfare broke out in the territory, the fort—which was never attacked—became a base for expeditions to subdue the hostile tribes. Then the frontier passed. The Plains Indians were sub-

dued, and in 1890 Fort Laramie was abandoned. Today it is a unit in the National Park System. Fort William and Fort John have completely disappeared, but the visitor can still see many of the buildings of the Army's Fort Laramie and visualize through them the appearance of a typical unfortified "fort" of the West.

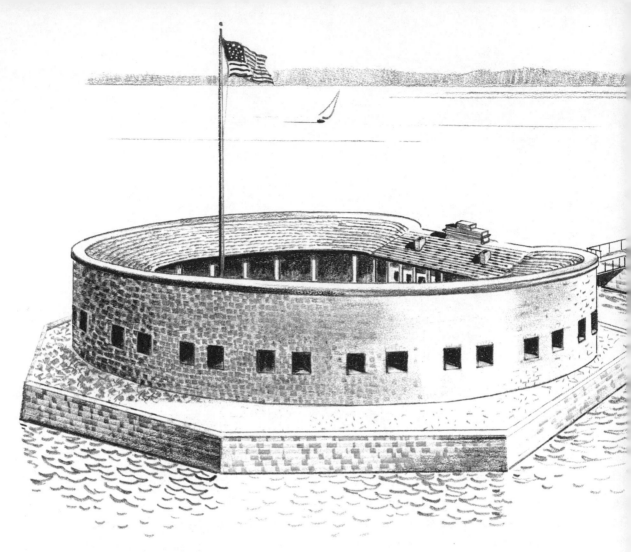

Defending the Coasts

Hostile Indians in the West were not the only problem facing the American Army. There was also the long coastline to defend against possible attack by an unfriendly European power. In the years immediately following the Revolution the new nation did not worry greatly about a threat from abroad. Then the troubles leading to the War of 1812 made Americans aware of the need for seacoast protection.

Coastal fortification was quite different from inland defense. For one thing, the enemy would probably be on shipboard. Most of the time the ships would be moving, and usually they would stay a long distance off. If the fort was on the mainland, an enemy might be able to land some distance away and attack on foot. Thus the land face of a seacoast fort might need a ravelin and bastions or some other device for a flanking fire

50

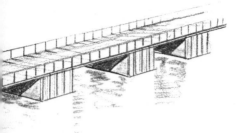

Castle Clinton

against assaulting troops. But the sea faces could be designed specifically to fight ships. This meant long rows of heavy cannon that could be swung in wide arcs to follow a moving vessel. Bastions would get in the way for such work, and so they were usually omitted. And since guns on moving ships could seldom hit twice in exactly the same spot, the solid walls of the land forts could be lightened. Indeed they could be hollowed out to make a series of rooms called casemates for mounting more cannon. Thus, instead of just having cannon on top of the ramparts like the old bastioned forts, new seacoast defenses might have two or even three tiers of guns.

Some of the earliest of these specialized seacoast forts were round or almost round. Castle Clinton, on a little man-made island 200 feet from the tip of Manhattan, had red sandstone walls 8 feet thick with one tier of casemates for guns. A timber causeway with a drawbridge connected it to the shore. Opposite, on Governors Island, stood another round tower, Castle William, with three tiers of guns. Both forts were begun as tension mounted with England, and were finished just before the War of 1812 actually broke out. Both are standing today. Castle William is still in use by the Army. Castle Clinton served as headquarters for the defenses of New York City and vicinity until 1821. Then it became in turn a place of amusement called Castle Gardens, an emigrant landing depot, the New York City Aquarium, and now Castle Clinton National Monument. Restored to its appearance as a fort, it stands in Battery Park surrounded by land reclaimed from the harbor.

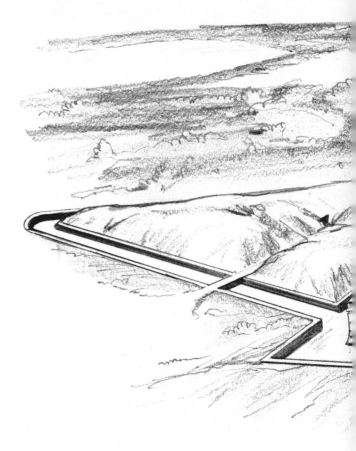

Fort Pulaski

FORT PULASKI After the War of 1812 the building of coastal forts began in earnest. Experience in the war had shown how weakly the shoreline was defended. At the direction of Congress a military board of engineers surveyed the entire coast and planned a series of forts from Maine to Florida and along the Gulf Coast to the mouth of the Mississippi River. For more than thirty years soldiers and civilians, masons and carpenters worked to complete the plan. The forts were excellent but while they were being built, weapons improved, and their first major tests found them obsolete.

Fort Pulaski was a prime example. Brigadier General Simon Bernard selected the site guarding the approaches to Savannah, Georgia, and made the preliminary plans for the fortifications. Bernard had been one of Napoleon's best military engineers and had come to America after the

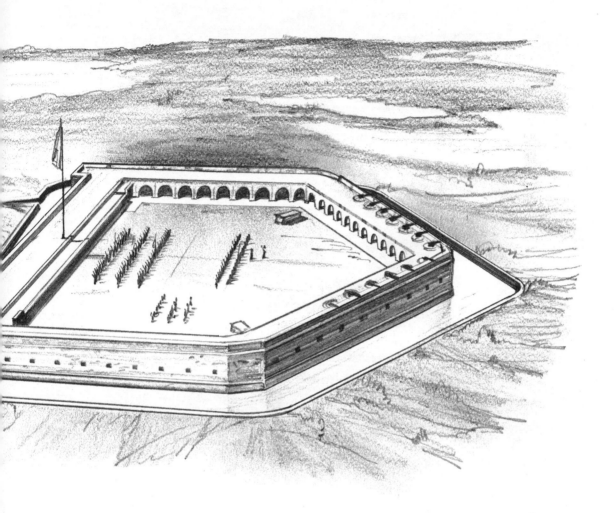

Battle of Waterloo to work on the board of engineers. Robert E. Lee, just graduated from the U. S. Military Academy at West Point, worked on the fort from 1829 to 1831 and so did other distinguished military engineers until it was finally finished in 1847.

Fort Pulaski was a big five-sided fort costing almost a million dollars to build. The land face with the drawbridge and entrance had little demi-bastions to provide flanking fire. There was also a ravelin and a wide wet moat on all sides. The solid brick walls were 7 to 11 feet thick and 32 feet high. There was one tier of casemates for cannon, and another tier of guns could be mounted on top. In all, plans called for 140 cannon to arm the massive masonry structure, but at the outbreak of the Civil War only 20 were in place.

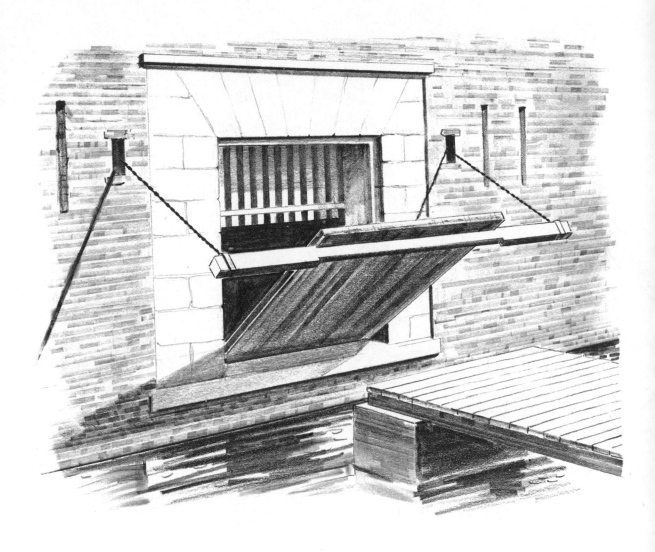

*Portcullis and drawbridge
at Fort Pulaski*

On April 11, 1862, Fort Pulaski came under fire for the first and only time. Southern troops had seized the fort just before the outbreak of war and they began immediately to prepare it for a defense. A Union force moved south to attack, but the Confederates were confident. "You might as well cannonade the Rocky Mountains as Fort Pulaski," declared one high military official. Eight hundred yards was considered the greatest distance from which cannon fire could knock down masonry walls, and the Yankees could not get that close. But the Southerners had not counted on the new rifled cannon. The Union forces set up a battery of these guns more than sixteen hundred yards away. From these guns shot weighing as much as 84 pounds apiece shattered the masonry. Within two days great holes had been punched in the massive walls, forcing the Confederates to surrender. Both sides were astonished at the ease with which the destruction had been accomplished. "The result of this bombardment must cause a change in the construction of fortifications," exulted Union General David Hunter. "No works of stone or brick can resist the impact of rifled artillery of heavy calibre."

Wall of Fort Pulaski after Union bombardment

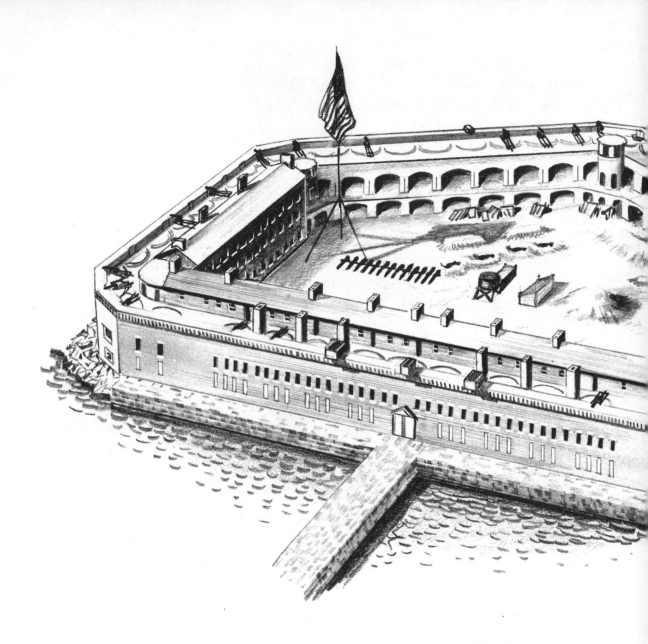

FORT
SUMTER   Fort Sumter in South Carolina reinforced this opinion and pointed the way for new developments. Like Pulaski, Sumter was a five-sided brick fort. Its walls towered some 48 feet above the waters of Charleston harbor with space for mounting three tiers of cannon. Since it stood on a man-made island and seemed to rise right out of the water, it needed no ravelin or bastions for defense against assault. It could only be attacked by artillery fire or by boats. Work on the fort had begun in 1829, and it was essentially completed in 1860 .

Within a year it received its first test of battle. The very first action of the Civil War was the bombardment of Fort Sumter on April 12, 1861.

Fort Sumter just before the Civil War

Confederate forces ringing the harbor opened fire on the fort from all sides. Short of ammunition and supplies, the Union garrison surrendered the next day after sustaining a bombardment of some 3,000 shots. The fort itself was not badly damaged although several fires started by shells had destroyed the barracks and threatened the powder magazine. The Confederates quickly repaired the damage.

Two years later the real test came. On April 7, 1863, nine Union iron-clad warships steamed past the fort and battered it with their guns for two hours and twenty minutes. Sumter's walls were scarred and battered, but the attack failed. Moreover, the defenders had succeeded in sinking one of the ships and disabling 5 others.

Confederate mortar battery fires on Fort Sumter

Foiled in this attempt, the Union troops were more determined than ever to take Fort Sumter. In August, 1863, they set up a battery of rifled cannon like the one that had conquered Fort Pulaski. They even put the same man in charge of it and gave him more and bigger guns. But the Confederates were determined. They filled the casemates with sand and cotton bales, making the walls solid, and they piled more sand, dirt and cotton inside and out. As fast as the Union guns knocked down a portion of the wall, the defenders built it up again with soft materials. For twenty-two months Sumter withstood both bombardment and direct assault. Federal cannon hurled more than 3,500 tons of shot and shell into it.

As a masonry fort it was a complete ruin, but it was stronger defensively than ever. The thick piles of dirt, sand and cotton over a core of brick and stone had produced walls that were virtually indestructible.

Both Fort Pulaski and Fort Sumter are preserved as units in the National Park System. The breach in the walls at Pulaski was repaired soon after the bombardment, but great holes in the masonry still attest to the power of the rifled guns which made them. Fort Sumter also was repaired and used after the Civil War. The walls have been lowered; the dirt has been cleared away from the outside, and there is a coast defense battery of 1899 in the midst of the old fort. It is now an interesting combination of early and recent coastal defenses, but there is still much to see of one of the most gallantly defended forts in American history.

Fort Sumter pointed the way to the future. Artillery was now too powerful for exposed masonry even in seacoast defenses; but masonry protected by a heavy layer of dirt would stand up against any known

The inside of Fort Sumter in 1865

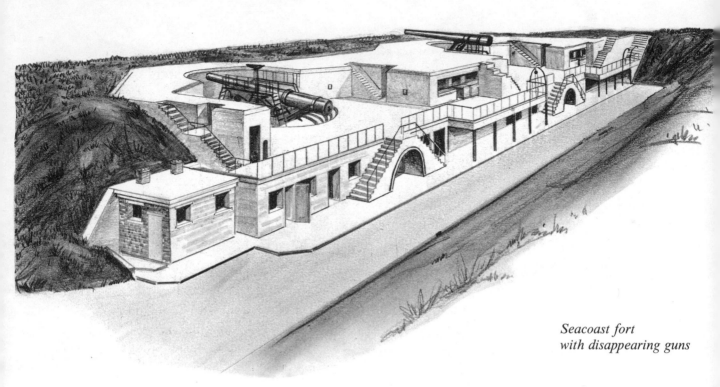

*Seacoast fort
with disappearing guns*

weapon. New forts would be dug into the ground or built as low hills. Developments in artillery helped also. Carriages were designed that could be raised and lowered so that a gun could suddenly appear over the top of the fort to fire, then drop down below thick walls of dirt and reinforced concrete for reloading. These were the famous "disappearing" guns of the late 1800's. Other cannon were designed to fire through narrow slits. The new coastal forts were hard to see from a distance, and they did not look very impressive, but they were infinitely stronger than the huge masonry structures of the years before the Civil War.

The United States built very few new coast defenses in the years right after the Civil War. Then the Spanish-American War of 1898 renewed in-

*Cross section of a seacoast fortification
of World War II*

terest in seacoast forts. A widespread fear that the Spanish fleet might attack cities along the Eastern seaboard started a rush to build new dirt and concrete forts. The Spanish-American War lasted only a few months, but the building of forts continued into the early 1900's. Every important harbor had coastal defense batteries. Most of these fortifications were soon abandoned, but a few seacoast defenses were still being built just before World War II.

These newest forts usually have a thick layer of dirt on top as well as in front for protection against air attack, but the defensive theory is still the same: give the enemy as little as possible to shoot at and use a soft material to absorb the force of his projectiles. It is the same theory, in fact, that has guided military engineers ever since cannon first proved high stone walls to be vulnerable.

The French had had these thoughts in mind when they built their low dirt walls at Fort Caroline. Four hundred years had brought changes in many aspects of design and function. Intricate systems of outworks to hold an enemy at bay had been devised. New building materials such as reinforced concrete had been developed. Infinitely more powerful and longer ranging weapons had appeared to attack. But these principles had held good. America's newest forts and her oldest are united in the same tradition, a tradition that has stood the test of time and proved sound.

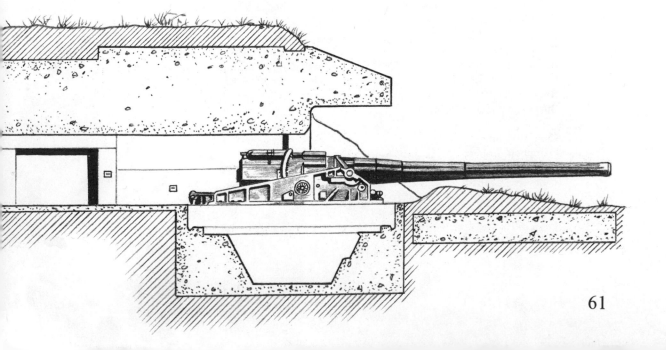

INDEX